CHARACTER COUNTS!

A Parent's Guide to
Preparing Your Child to Make Good Choices

Written by Q. L. Pearce

Illustrated by Roberta Collier-Morales,
Cheryl Nobens, Len Shalansky, Tani Brooks Johnson,
Cary Pillo Lassen, and Jenny Campbell
Cover illustration by Roberta Collier-Morales

BV15040 A Parent's Guide to Developing Character in Your Preschooler
Printed in Canada
Published by Brighter Vision Publications
225 Duncan Mill Road
Don Mills, Ontario, Canada M3B 3K9

TM is a trademark of Brighter Vision Publications.

CONTENTS

My Posters include: (above with ✳ and ...)

Integrity
Perseverance

CHARACTER COUNTS!℠

INTRODUCTION

by Michael Josephson, President, CHARACTER COUNTS℠ Coalition

Character is what a person is inside. Our character is revealed by how we act when we think no one else is looking. It is how we treat people who we think cannot help or hurt us. A person of character has good ethical values that distinguish right from wrong, and a strong commitment to do what is right even when it is inconvenient, uncomfortable or personally costly. Character, in short, is moral strength.

Good character does not develop spontaneously. Rather, it is the result of conscientious efforts to instill and reinforce ethical values in a way that makes them second nature. This sense of right and wrong is referred to as the conscience. Conscience is the moral compass of character.

This book is organized around the Six Pillars of Character℠, a character development framework developed by the CHARACTER COUNTS℠ Coalition, an alliance of hundreds of leading educational, youth-serving, and community organizations dedicated to strengthening the character of youth. The Six Pillars of Character℠ are trustworthiness, respect, responsibility, fairness, caring, and citizenship.

A Parent's Guide to Developing Character in Your Preschooler is divided into six sections, with each dedicated to a specific character trait. The sections provide information about the trait,

suggestions for modeling it to your child, and ideas for helping your child understand and incorporate the trait into his or her own thinking and behavior.

Effective character education involves encouraging and reinforcing habits that form internal mechanisms of control and moral courage. Character education is necessary to help children develop the tools and strategies they need to make moral choices they can be proud of. A parent can provide no greater gift.

Preschoolers and Character

By preschool age, most youngsters are capable of understanding the difference between good and bad behavior. This is the time when many parents introduce their children to the concept of morality.

To teach children we must be clear about our own values. The Six Pillars of Character℠ offer shared beliefs and consensus values that transcend culture and religion. Trustworthiness, respect, responsibility, fairness, caring and citizenship are core values in society that can be reinforced by parents, teachers, coaches, religious leaders, and other community members as your child develops basic ethical standards.

Your Three-Year-Old

By age three, youngsters can begin to understand basic concepts of right and wrong. It is the perfect time to equip your youngster with the tools and language needed to develop sound moral character.

Your three-year-old is growing emotionally and socially. As your child moves from the self-centered toddler stage, he will now learn to take turns, play in a group, follow simple structured activities, and "help out" around the house in small ways. It's a good time to nurture the beginnings of responsibility. The aspects of fairness and caring become important as your child enters preschool and engages in cooperative play with a variety of children. At this age, children often imitate their parents as a way of "trying on" new behaviors. Be sure to model the behaviors you wish to see.

Your Four-Year-Old

Most four-year-olds seem to enjoy the company of friends, and often engage in loosely organized games such as tag. It is a time for testing limits. Four-year-olds may exhibit growing self-confidence to the point of defiance. Your child may push for more freedom of choice, and she is old enough to learn that with choice, comes responsibility. In addition, a basic understanding of respect for herself and for others is an important part of character development in your child's expanding social environment.

As your child interacts with others, you can't expect her to always avoid conflict. She will need tools to help settle disagreements in the best way, and to deal with disappointment—all aspects of respect.

Your Five-Year-Old

At five, your child probably has a "best friend," is capable of playing a simple board game, shows pride in accomplishments, and wants to take on more responsibility (such as caring for a pet). This is also the age at which children learn the difference between fact and fiction. Your child may lie to please you or avoid punishment. If so, you can emphasize the trait of trustworthiness. Modeling is particularly important. Don't ask your child to tell a caller on the phone that you are not at home, or lie about your child's age to pay a lower entrance fee to an event.

Your five-year-old will also begin to exhibit increasing interest in his community and environment. Stress the importance of being a good citizen. Explain how everyone within a community is connected.

Developing Character
using the T.E.A.M. strategy

The T.E.A.M. strategy, developed by the CHARACTER COUNTS℠ Coalition, is an effective approach for helping our children have strong values and good character.

Teach

Teach your child that his or her character counts—that personal success and happiness will depend on who your child is on the inside, not what he or she has or how he or she looks. Tell your child that people of character know the difference between right and wrong because they guide their thoughts and actions by six basic rules of living (the Six Pillars of Character℠)—trustworthiness, respect, responsibility, fairness, caring, and good citizenship. Explain the meaning of these words. Use examples from your own life, history, and the news.

Enforce

Instill the Six Pillars of Character℠ by rewarding good behavior (usually praise is enough) and by discouraging all instances of bad behavior by imposing (or, in some cases, allowing others to impose) fair, consistent consequences that prove you are serious about character. Demonstrate courage and firmness of will by enforcing the core values when it is difficult or costly to do so. Character building is most effective when you regularly see and seize opportunities to

1) Build your child's awareness of the moral importance of his or her choices.
2) Increase your child's desire to do the right thing.
3) Help your child strengthen his or her ability to think about the consequences of choices, consider alternative behaviors, and do the right thing.

Advocate

Continuously encourage your child to live up to the Six Pillars of Character℠ in all his or her thoughts and actions. Be an advocate for character. Don't be neutral about the importance of character nor casual about improper conduct. Be clear and uncompromising in letting your child know that you want and expect him or her to be trustworthy, respectful, responsible, fair, caring, and a good citizen.

Model

Be careful and self-conscious about setting a good example in everything you say and do. Hold yourself to the highest standards of character by honoring the Six Pillars of Character℠ at all times. You may be a good model now, but remember, you don't have to be sick to get better. Everything you do, and don't do, sends a message about your values. Be sure your messages reinforce your lessons about doing the right thing even when it is hard to do so. When you slip (and most of us do), act the way you want your children to behave when they act improperly. Be accountable, apologize sincerely, and work to do better.

Meet the Characters

Trustworthiness

Shinrai the Camel represents trustworthiness. Her name is derived from the Japanese word for *trust*. Trustworthiness includes being reliable and loyal. Shinrai is steadfast and has the courage to do the right thing. She keeps her promises, always does what she says she will do, and is always on time. She wears a "true blue" ribbon.

Respect

Austus the Lion is respectful. His name is derived from the Estonian word for *respect*. Respect is using good manners and being considerate of the feelings of others. Austus is tolerant of differences and deals peacefully with disagreements. He would never tease or make fun of anyone. Austus follows the Golden Rule. He wears a yellow ribbon.

Responsibility

Ansvar's name is derived from the Norwegian word for *responsible*, and he's a responsible elephant. Responsibility means doing what you say you will and using self-control. Ansvar thinks before he acts and is accountable for his choices. He keeps his goals in mind, has a strong sense of duty, and is a first-class worker. He ties reminder ribbons around his tail and toes and plans carefully so that he can fulfill his responsibilities. He wears a green ribbon.

Fairness

Guisto the Giraffe is a symbol of fairness and his name is derived from the Italian word for *fair*. Fairness is playing by the rules, taking turns, and sharing. Guisto is open-minded and listens to others, even those whose viewpoints differ from his. He would never blame someone else unjustly. His ribbon is bright orange.

Caring

Karina the Kangaroo is caring. Her name is derived from the Spanish word for *caring*. A caring person is kind and compassionate. Karina expresses gratitude, forgives others, and helps those in need. She understands how others are feeling and considers how her actions or decisions might affect others. She'll do whatever she can to help a friend. Karina wears a red ribbon.

Citizenship

Kupa is derived from the Hawaiian word for *citizen*. Kupa the Bear is a good citizen. Citizenship includes doing your share to make the community better, and obeying laws and rules. Good citizens stay informed, vote, and work to protect the environment. Kupa is knowledgeable of history and other cultures. She respects authority and is a good neighbor.

Developing Trustworthiness

Trustworthiness is essential to building positive relationships with others. A trustworthy person is honest, reliable, loyal, and has integrity. People with integrity stand up for their beliefs. They live by their principles no matter what others say, and they have the courage to do what is right even when it's hard to do or failure might result.

There is a wise saying, "Complete honesty, even in little things, is not a little thing at all." Honesty means telling the truth, but it is more than that. An honest person is sincere and candid, and doesn't cheat, steal, or behave in a tricky or deceptive manner. Reliability is another important aspect of trustworthiness. Reliable people keep their promises, honor their words and commitments, are dependable, and do what they are supposed to do. A loyal person is a good friend, stands up for and protects family, friends, school and country, and keeps secrets.

Signs of Trustworthiness

Praise your child when he or she:

- Tells the truth knowing a punishment might result
- Is willing to try again even if she failed or didn't get the result she wanted
- Returns something that he has borrowed
- Gets ready for school on time
- Keeps a promise

Meet Shinrai the Camel

Introduce your child to Shinrai the Camel to help develop concepts about trustworthiness. Begin by showing Shinrai's picture, then encourage conversation with these questions and comments.

- What animal is this? She has a name. It is Shinrai. Can you say that?
- Shinrai stands for trustworthiness. That's a big word. Do you know what it means? Shinrai is trustworthy. That means she always keeps her promises. She always does what she says she will do and is always on time.
- It sounds like Shinrai would be a good friend, doesn't it? Well she is. She thinks that it's very important to treat friends nicely. One thing she would never do to her friends is lie to them. Can you tell me the difference between a truth and a lie? Lies can hurt people. Can you think of some ways that a lie might hurt someone?
- Look at Shinrai's ribbon. What color is it? That's right, it's blue. Shinrai is a true blue friend.

She wants to help you be your best self and teach you lots of things about trustworthiness. Let's learn some of them together.

Developing Trustworthiness

Modeling Trustworthiness

It is important that you model trustworthiness for your child and that you point out trustworthy behavior to your child.

- Set an example of reliability by returning things that you borrow promptly, and arriving on time for appointments.
- Have your child sit beside you for a few moments while you are paying bills. Explain that a check is like a promise. You owe money to someone for a service, and you are now making good on your promise to pay.
- Don't betray a trust, but explain that there are times when you have to stand up for what's right even if it means upsetting a friend. For example, don't let your friends hurt themselves, do anything wrong, or spread rumors or gossip.
- Never have your child lie for you. For example, don't ask your child to tell a phone caller that you are not home. This will send your child the message that you can't be trusted.

We Depend on the Honesty of Others

Explain to your child that lies can be hurtful and even dangerous. Work together to write a story or draw a picture about a town where everybody lies and cheats. Imagine what it might be like to go to the supermarket. How would you be able to tell if your purchases were weighed properly? Maybe a can labeled *Fruit* would really have boiled turnips inside. How would you know that the cashier is charging you correctly or giving you the right change? Ask your child what would happen if you wanted to go to the movies and someone had put all the wrong starting times on the marquee. You couldn't trust the telephone book to be correct, and a visit to the doctor could be dangerous if she said you were well when you were ill.

After you have finished your story or picture, discuss some of the ways that we must depend on others to tell the truth.

Developing Trustworthiness

Tower of Trust

Trust is something that is built up over time. Gather together wooden blocks, cereal boxes, or small cans. Sit together and build a tower from the objects. Start by building a solid foundation. Tell your youngster that building the tower is something like building trust. Trust is also based on a solid foundation of truth. Carefully build several more levels. Once you have a tall tower, explain that telling a lie is like pulling a block out of the foundation of the tower. Have your child pull out one block, then another until the tower falls.

Say that trust can crumble in the same way. Ask if the tower can be rebuilt. Point out that it can, but you have to start from the bottom by re-establishing the foundation. Talk about how lying undermines trust.

Promise Keeping at the Library

The public library provides an excellent opportunity for building trustworthiness in your child. Many libraries will issue a card to a child as soon as she can print her own name. If she is unable to do that, make one for her on a 3 x 5 index card. Perhaps you can glue on a picture of a camel to remind your child of Shinrai, the trustworthy camel. Use your card to check out the books from the public library and have your child check them out from you. Start with two. Explain that when you take out a book you have promised to keep it safe and return it at a certain time. Show your child the return date in the book. Find a special place in your home where she can keep her library books. Place a calendar with the books so she can see when they are due back. When the due date arrives, take your child along to return the books. Explain that a trustworthy person takes good care of library books so that they don't get ruined or lost, and she returns them on time.

Developing Trustworthiness

A Promise Star

Tell your child that a promise is not something to be made or taken lightly. Ask how she feels when someone makes a promise and doesn't keep it. Explain that simply forgetting is not an excuse, because a trustworthy person finds a way to remember. Help your child to remember by making a promise star. Cut a star shape about one inch high from cardboard. Have your child decorate it in any way she likes using glitter, stickers, or markers. You can get a simple tie-pin style back with a safety "pinch" style clasp on it at any craft store. Glue the pin to the back of the star. When your child makes a promise, ask her to wear the pin to help her remember.

Honest Abe

Tell your child about Abraham Lincoln. Look together at his image on a penny. Explain that he was the sixteenth president of the United States and that he was nicknamed "Honest Abe." He received the name because when a business he bought failed, he worked very hard to pay back the debts from that business. Ask your youngster if she would trust someone like Lincoln. Why? Help your child make a stovepipe hat like Lincoln's from a paper plate and construction paper. Cut the center out of a plate and use the remaining ring as the brim of the hat. Color the rim black. Roll a 9 x 12-inch sheet of black construction paper into a wide tube shape and tape it along the edge to form the stovepipe part of the hat. Tape the construction paper tube to the brim.

Loyal Friends

Demonstrate loyalty by maintaining connections with your own friends. Pick a time to sit down with your child and write notes to friends or family members who are far away. To make it more fun, have your youngster design and make notecards. Gather items such as construction paper, glue, colored markers, glitter, pictures from magazines, feathers, yarn, tissue paper and more. Fold a piece of construction paper in half widthwise, then cut it along the fold. Fold one of the cut pieces in half to form a notecard. Share a sweet or funny story or two about your relationship with the person you will write to, then ask your child to decorate the front of the notecard for that person. If your preschooler can print his name, he can also sign the note.

Developing Respect

A person of character values all persons, lives by the Golden Rule, respects the dignity, privacy, and freedom of others, is courteous and polite to all, and is tolerant and accepting of differences. Tolerance and acceptance are two key aspects of respect. Respectful people judge others on their character, abilities and conduct, not on race, religion, gender, where they live, how they dress, or the amount of money they have.

Respectful people are tolerant of those who are different. They listen to others and try to understand their point of view. A person who is respectful resolves disagreements, responds to insults, and handles feelings of anger peacefully.

Respecting others includes being courteous, polite and civil to everyone. The Golden Rule is a helpful guide when showing respect.

Signs of Respect

Praise your child when he or she:

- Doesn't interrupt when you are speaking
- Listens respectfully
- Asks permission before using something that belongs to another person
- Doesn't join in when someone is being teased
- Uses good manners
- Is polite

Table Manners
*See A-beka Community Helpers Book
*Creative Correction Book – not interrupting idea

Meet Austus the Lion

Introduce your child to Austus to help develop concepts about respect. Begin by showing this picture of Austus, then encourage conversation with these questions and comments.

- This is Austus. He is a lion and he stands for respect. He thinks that it is very important to have respect for oneself, and for others. Can you think of ways to show respect?
- Lions are strong aren't they? Austus may be strong, but he would

rather settle disagreements nicely instead of fighting or calling mean names. That's because he has respect for everyone, even those who don't agree with him.

- Austus shows respect by being polite and by using good manners. He would never tease or make fun of anyone.
- Look at Austus' coat and his pretty ribbon. What color are they? They are golden-yellow, the color of the Golden Rule. Do you know what that is? The Golden Rule says that you should treat people the way you want to be treated. Do you think the world would be a nice place if everyone lived by that rule?

Developing Respect

Modeling Respect

Your child will learn how to treat people by watching how you treat people. Be a good model of respectful behavior!

- Show respect to your child by spending time with him, listening to his ideas, and speaking to him in a respectful manner.
- Remember that your child often hears adult conversations. Speak respectfully of others, even if the person being discussed is not a friend. Avoid stereotypes or labels based on race. Don't tell or laugh at jokes that are at the expense of someone else. Help your child understand that intolerance is generally based not on reality, but on perception.
- Be respectful of the elderly. Many cultures revere their aged and the term *elder* is generally a term of respect. Teach your child that seniors have valuable experience and many have great stories to tell.
- Take good care of property you are allowed to use and don't take or use property without permission.

We're Alike and Different

Here is a way for your child to learn about acceptance and get to know his friends a little better at the same time. Have your child sit with one or two friends on the floor. Place a large stack of old magazines between them and a paper bag in front of them. Have the children go through the magazines and tear out pictures of things that they like. For example, your child may put in a picture of a pizza, a dog, or a park. When the children are finished, go through the bag and hold up each picture. Ask the children to raise their hand if they like it. If it is unanimous, put the picture in one pile. If not, put it in another. The youngsters may be surprised to find out how many likes they have in common. When they have finished, help them to think of other ways they are alike and different. Note that people come in different colors, shapes and sizes, and from different types of families, but they can always find some things they have in common, and accept those things that are different.

Developing Respect

A Garden of Good Manners

Good manners and courtesy are tools of respect. Explain to your child that he has many choices when it comes to using respectful language. For this activity you will need red construction paper cut into tulip shapes, crayons or markers, and a large piece of construction paper for a background. With your child, think up as many polite words or phrases as you can.

Examples: thank you, please, how do you do?, may I?, pardon me, after you, excuse me. Write the words or phrases on the tulips. Direct your child to glue the tulips to the background paper, leaving room to draw stems. Then let your child draw stems and leaves for each tulip. Tell your child that he has created a garden of good manners and he can use these "flowers" any time.

Teddy Bear Tea

This activity is for a group of four or more. Invite a few of your child's friends to a "teddy bear tea." Each child should bring a favorite teddy bear. Have the children sit in a circle with the bears in their laps. One at a time, each bear comes up with something nice to say about the person sitting on the left, then whispers it to his child, who says it aloud. Pretending that the bears are getting the ideas helps each child to express herself more freely. Once everyone has had a turn, repeat the activity by saying something nice about the person on the right. When the game is over, set out the tea party and remind the children to set a good example for their bears by using courtesy and good manners. This activity helps children practice finding nice things to say to each other and gives them an opportunity to practice good manners.

My Manners Mat

Learning table manners is a good way for a preschooler to gain confidence. The placemat she makes in this activity will help her to think of manners, then get a gentle reminder at each meal. You'll need a piece of heavy white paper (9 x 12 or larger), crayons, and clear self-adhesive plastic sheets used to line shelves. On a separate piece of paper, help your child to make a list of things to remember at the table. This could include: chew with your mouth closed; no elbows on the table; don't reach; and thank the cook. When the list is finished, write the items on the white paper and have your child draw a picture to go with each one. When she has completed her work, seal the mat between two sheets of clear self-adhesive plastic.

Developing Character in Your Preschooler

Developing Respect

Managing Anger

A respectful person does not use violence to settle conflicts. To help your child learn to resolve conflicts calmly, rehearse alternatives to violence. Ask your child to think of things that make her feel angry. How does she usually act when she is angry? Explain that yelling or hitting in response might feel satisfying, but that they do not show respect for herself or for others. Remind your child that you expect her to express her anger in safe and respectful ways. Help her to make a pair of finger puppets that she can use to practice what to do and say when something angers her. Draw two figures on construction paper about two inches high, then cut them out. Have your child add details with a marker. Cut out two 2-inch-long by 1/2-inch-wide paper strips. Form rings and tape the ends. Tape one puppet to each ring.

You Can't Judge a Gift by Its Wrapping

Explain to your youngster that it is wrong to judge people by where they live, how they dress, and how much money they have. Point out that what is in a person's heart, how a person behaves, and how a person treats others are all more important. Here is a fun way to demonstrate this concept. Gather four small boxes of the same size. Put dirt or sand in one, pebbles in another, bolts in the third and your child's favorite candy in the last. Wrap each one differently. Make the candy box the least attractive. Let your child choose a package and open it. When he is finished have him open the rest of the packages. Ask if he was surprised by the contents of the boxes. Help your child understand that just like he couldn't tell what was inside the packages by looking at the outside wrappings, you can't always tell what people are like inside by how they look on the outside.

We Can Compromise

Explain the meaning of compromise—an agreement between two or more people in which both sides give in a little to reach a settlement somewhere in the middle. Suggest a scenario in which two children both want an apple, but there is only one left. Ask your child what sort of compromise would make both children happy. She might say the apple could be cut in half. They could also make apple sauce. If she would like to try again, suggest that two children want to share a pretty flowering plant. How can they do that without harming the plant?

Developing Responsibility

Responsible people understand two key concepts. First, life is full of choices. Second, we are in charge of our choices. With these concepts as a foundation, a responsible person knows and does his or her duty, is accountable, pursues excellence, and exercises self-control.

Doing one's duty means acknowledging and meeting legal and moral obligations. This includes following laws, keeping commitments, fulfilling job responsibilities, and so on. People who are accountable accept responsibility for their choices. Before they act, they think about the consequences to themselves and others. Accountable people also think long-term and do what they can to make things better.

Responsible people pursue excellence. They work hard and make all they do worthy of pride. They set realistic goals and persevere as they pursue those goals. Finally, responsible people know that although something is legal and accepted in society, it may not be morally correct. They know the difference between what they have the right to do and what is right to do.

Signs of Responsibility

Praise your child when he or she:

- Completes an assigned chore without complaint
- Achieves a goal
- Admits to a mistake and doesn't try to blame anyone else
- Apologizes when wrong
- Keeps a commitment
- Works hard

Meet Ansvar the Elephant

Introduce your child to Ansvar to help develop concepts about responsibility. Begin by showing this picture of Ansvar, then encourage conversation with these questions and comments.

- This is Ansvar the elephant. He stands for responsibility. Try to say that word. What are some responsibilities that you have?

- Ansvar has a bow tied around his trunk. Can you guess what that is for? It is to help him remember things that he is supposed to do. Some people say that elephants never forget, but Ansvar wants to be sure because he takes his responsibilities very seriously. What are other things he can

do to help him remember? How about writing a To Do list?

- When Ansvar makes plans, he thinks about how his actions will affect others. He always does his best, but when Ansvar's plans don't work out, he doesn't try to blame anyone else. He thinks hard about the things that he did or didn't do that led to the problem.

- Ansvar is a first-class worker and he wants to help you develop good work habits, too.

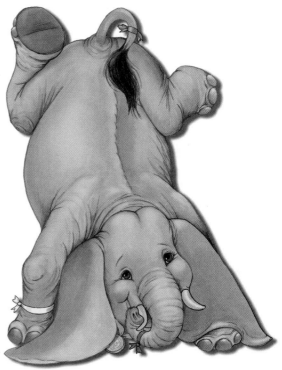

Developing Responsibility

Modeling Responsibility

Point out to your child that all people have responsibilities to themselves, their families, their neighbors, their employers, and their communities. Some are personal and some are shared.

- Brainstorm about some of those responsibilities and explain why they are important. Tax time offers a good opportunity to model duty. As you work on your taxes, point out what types of community services the taxes support.
- Avoid making excuses or blaming others when you make a mistake. Let your child see that you are accountable for your own choices whether they have large or small consequences.
- Apologize when you are wrong. If you are not afraid to say you are sorry, your child won't be either.
- Practice self-control. Don't yell at a referee during sporting events or call another driver a name while on the road.

Setting a Goal

Ask your child if he knows what it means to set a goal. Talk about goals you have set and the steps you took to achieve them. They could be educational goals, career goals, financial goals, health-related goals, and so on. Then talk with your child about something he or she would like to achieve. It can be a skill such as riding a bike, a purchase such as buying a toy, or some other goal. Discuss the goal with your child. Is it realistic or is it a goal which may have to be achieved when your child is older? Either way, help your child identify steps he or she could take now to achieve the goal. Explain that some goals can be met in a short time. For example, your child may want to finish coloring a picture before bedtime. Other goals, such as learning to swim, can take a while to achieve.

Developing Responsibility

"Turn Around" Talk

Remind your child that a responsible person doesn't give up. Brainstorm together to come up with a list of "give up" phrases. Examples: It is too hard to pick up my toys after I play with them, I am too little to help take care of my pet, I can't remember my numbers, I'll never learn to count.

Work together to come up with "turn around" phrases. Examples: I can do it; I'll try; This isn't as hard as I thought. When your child starts using "give up" phrases, gently encourage him or her to think about a "turn around" phrase instead.

Doing My Part

Even very young children can handle some responsibilities in the form of chores. On a large posterboard, make a family chores chart. Create a column for every family member, including your preschooler. Label each column at the top with the person's name. Let your child decorate the poster with colored markers. Gather together as a family to fill in the chores. Some entries for your preschooler could be wash hands before dinner, pick up toys, fill pet's water bowl, brush teeth, make bed, and so on.

JOBS

Mom	Dad	Betsy	Max
Laundry	Mow Lawn	Sort socks	Brush Teeth
Dishes		make bed	
Shop	Wash Car	set table	wash hands
Dust			
Vacuum	Take out Trash	Brush teeth	feed Spot
Scrub		wash hands	
Cook	Cook	give Spot a bath	pick up toys
Drive Kids to Dance and Soccer	Rake		Share
	Weed Yard and garden	feed Tweety	comb hair
		water plants	

Just Rewards

A person of character lives up to his or her responsibilities without thinking of being rewarded. Still, sometimes a job well done calls for a treat. On occasion, you might like to encourage your child if she is reluctant to complete a task. One "sweet" way is to

set out a cupcake with a layer of icing on top. Use gel icing (available in most supermarkets) to write a description of the chore on the cupcake. For example, write "dust dollhouse" in gel icing. When the chore is done, your child can eat the cupcake.

Developing Character in Your Preschooler

Developing Responsibility

Television as a Teacher

Edward R. Murrow said of television that it could "be an instrument which can teach, illuminate and inspire." Responsible television watching can be fun for you and your child, as well as a good teaching opportunity. Choose a television show that is age-appropriate. Record the program if possible so that you can pause or rewind it as you like. Settle into a comfortable chair with your child beside you and watch the show together. Pause the tape now and then to ask questions or make comments about how characters handle certain situations. Ask your child if she agrees with what the character did, or if she would do something different. If you are watching a cartoon and some of the characters hit others, point out that in real life, violence is never acceptable, and usually results in someone getting hurt.

My Own Phone Book

Self-reliance is an important element of responsibility. Being able to get help in an emergency is a life-saving skill that most preschoolers can master. Help your child to prepare his own telephone book to use, even if he is unable to read. Ask him who he would like to include in the book and obtain photos of each person. Suggest that a neighbor of his choice should also be included. Write each person's number in the notebook in large, clear printing. Glue or tape the appropriate photograph next to the number. Write the number for the police and fire department as well. Add a picture of a fireman and policeman cut from a magazine. On the front cover of the book write your home phone number and address. Tape your child's photo next to it. Below that write 911 in very large numbers. Explain that 911 is for emergencies and discuss what might be an emergency. Let your child decorate his book and keep it near the telephone.

Developing Fairness

A person of character is fair and just. To be fair means to treat people equally and to make decisions based on proper considerations, without favoritism or prejudice. People who are fair are careful when making judgments about others. They try to listen impartially and hear the facts with an open mind before forming opinions. They listen openly to opposing viewpoints.

Fair people don't take more than their share, don't take advantage of others, and don't blame others for something they didn't do. They follow fair procedures. Fair people impose consequences for misbehavior that are proportional to the wrongdoing (not too harsh or too lenient).

While it is sometimes difficult to determine a fair course of action, most people can easily identify when a situation is unfair. A person of character works hard to avoid being unfair.

Signs of Fairness
Praise your child when he or she:
- Takes turns with other children
- Shares a toy
- Plays a game by the rules
- Listens attentively to another person's point of view
- Accepts consequences of misbehavior

Meet Guisto the Giraffe

Introduce your child to Guisto to help develop concepts about fairness. Begin by showing Guisto's picture; then encourage conversation with these comments and questions:

- This animal's name is Guisto. What kind of animal is he?
- Guisto stands for fairness. He is wise and graceful and always tries to do what is right.
- Look at his long neck. Do you think he can see things that are far away? I know something else Guisto can see. From way up high he can always see both sides of a story, and he has a nice way of helping others to do the same.

- Guisto plays by the rules because that is fair. Do you think it would be fun to play a game with Guisto? What kind of games do you think he might be good at? I'll bet whenever he plays, he always waits for his turn and is happy to share. Guisto knows that in life everything isn't always fair—but he believes that we can be fair.

Developing Fairness

Modeling Fairness

Your children will learn about fairness by watching how you act in a variety of situations. Of course, how you treat your children will have a significant influence. How you make other choices related to fairness will also have an impact on your child's thinking.

- Give your child the opportunity to have a voice in family decisions whenever possible. For example, family members could take turns choosing group leisure time activities.
- Listen carefully to your child's explanation of a situation before jumping to conclusions about what happened.
- Be sure that your expectations were clear before disciplining your child.
- Help your children understand the complexities of fairness. For example, in a family game of softball, it may be fair for the pitcher to move closer to home plate when a young child is up at bat.
- Make an effort to treat all your children equitably, even if you favor one over the others. This will have a lasting impact on their relationships with you and with one another.

A Sharing Box

An early skill that preschoolers can learn is sharing. Let your child know that sharing is a good thing, but she doesn't have to share everything. For example, if a friend comes over to visit, there may be some toys that she would rather not let her guest use. It's fair to make those toys off limits to everyone while the guest is present. Work with your child to identify toys that she is willing to share. You may wish to fill a sharing box with such toys. It could include coloring books, crayons and craft supplies, as well as selected toys. Further develop concepts about sharing by helping your child identify things that family members share. For example, furniture, dishes, the television, the yard, and so on.

One Cuts, the Other Chooses

If you are having difficulty with siblings who feel that they are not treated fairly when it comes to treats, here is a way to stop some of the bickering. Imagine, for example, that the children each want a nice chewy brownie, but there is only one left. How can they cut it so that both children feel they are being treated fairly? Allow one child to do the cutting. Allow the other child to choose the piece he wants. This will ensure that the child who does the cutting makes the pieces as equal as possible.

Developing Character in Your Preschooler

Developing Fairness

Rules Are Fair

Ask your child if he knows why rules are important. Explain that rules are made to protect people, to protect property, and to ensure that people are treated fairly. Talk with your child about rules that ensure fairness, such as taking turns. What would happen if people did not take turns using equipment, playing a game, or while at a stop sign? Explain that in your home some rules are the same for everyone and others are not. For example, everyone has to use good table manners. However, if there are children of different ages in the house, older siblings probably go to bed later. They may also be able to go out alone. Another example is that you can use sharp knives, but your preschooler is probably not allowed to. Help your preschooler understand that fair doesn't always mean equal.

Share the Work and the Results

Making ice cream is a delicious way to demonstrate fairness by sharing the work to enjoy a treat. You can do this with one child or more. You will need a small, clean coffee can with a lid, and a large coffee can with a lid, ice, rock salt, 1 cup of milk, 1 cup of heavy cream, 1/2 cup of sugar and 1/2 teaspoon of vanilla. All ingredients should be very cold. Place the milk, cream, sugar, and vanilla in the small can, then put the small can inside the large can. Fill the space between the two cans with ice and about 1/2 cup of rock salt.

Have the children sit on the floor and roll the can back and forth to each other for at least twenty minutes while singing songs or playing counting games. At the end of that time, check to see if ice cream is forming on the side of the can. If so, scrape off a taste for each child. Explain that making ice cream takes a lot of work, but it's easier if everyone shares. Then of course, everyone gets to share the treat.

Developing Fairness

An Expanding World

You can combat prejudicial attitudes before they have a chance to develop by providing your child with opportunities to be around people of varying backgrounds and cultures.

- Watch for opportunities to participate in community events that feature various cultures.
- Model openness and appreciation of the differences between groups of people.
- Ask your children's librarian to recommend age-appropriate storybooks about children from varying ethnic and cultural backgrounds.
- If you live in a highly homogenous community, you can expand your child's world by attending events in more heterogenous communities. For example, if you live in a rural suburban area, you might attend children's museum workshops in an urban area.

Careful Judgments

It is important that you speak fairly about people from varying ethnic groups. Help your child understand that it is unfair to judge anyone by the actions of someone else. Every person must be judged based on his or her own individual merit. You might wish to make a game of this by telling your child this story. *Let's pretend you met a girl wearing a green dress. Imagine that she was* *mean and would never share her toys. Does that mean that everyone who wears a green dress is mean?* Help your child understand that the only way to know if someone is mean is to observe his or her own behavior. It is unfair to assume that just because someone looks or dresses like someone else, that they will behave in the same way.

Fair Access

Next time you and your child are enjoying a public place, such as a beach, library, or park, ask your child this question: *Would it be fair if only people with brown eyes and brown hair were allowed to come here? Why not?* Talk with your child about the inequity of having rules that discriminate against certain people because of how they look. (As you feel it is appropriate for your child, you can develop this further by talking about the civil rights movement in the U.S.) Another time (perhaps the next time you are at the market), point out and talk with your child about parking spaces that are reserved for handicapped people. Help your child understand that it is fair for handicapped persons to have parking spaces that are closer to entrances because they have physical limitations that others do not have.

Developing Caring

People who are caring feel a genuine concern for the well-being of others. They are kind, loving, considerate, and charitable. A caring person puts himself or herself in another person's shoes, and responds with compassion to the needs of others.

Caring people are grateful and appreciative of the kindnesses shown to them by others. They find ways to forgive others for their shortcomings.

A caring person has a charitable spirit and is generous to those in need. Caring people give money, time, support, and comfort, just for the sake of making someone else's life better, not for praise, gratitude, or some other external reward. They are never too busy to help out or lend a hand.

Signs of Caring

Praise your child when he or she:

- Shows concern for the feelings of another
- Asks you how you are feeling
- Exhibits patience
- Remembers to thank someone for being kind
- Offers to help
- Treats any living thing gently

Meet Karina the Kangaroo

Introduce your child to Karina to help develop concepts about caring. Begin by showing Karina's picture; then encourage conversation with these comments and questions:

- Karina is a special kangaroo. She is very caring. She is always aware of how others are feeling, like when they are hungry, or sad, or scared.
- Karina has a special pocket called a pouch. What do real kangaroos carry in their pouches? Karina carries things that people might need. She does that because she cares.
- What sort of things do you think she carries in her pouch?

What could she carry to help someone who was sad?

- Karina always thinks about how an action or decision might affect someone else. Karina would never be mean or try to hurt someone's feelings.
- She'll do whatever she can to help a friend, and she never forgets to say thank you when someone helps her.

Being kind makes Karina feel warm and happy inside.

Developing Caring

Modeling Caring

Modeling caring to your child, your family and friends, and to strangers, will provide an invaluable example to your youngster. In addition, as your child feels cared for and loved, he or she will be better able to show love.

- Be affectionate with your youngster. Hold and hug him regularly. Read a story with your arm around your child and his head on your shoulder. Tuck him into bed.
- When your child is having a "bad day" listen to what's troubling her. When you are having a "bad day" give your child the opportunity to help you by listening to an age-appropriate version of what worries you.
- Let your child see you giving generously of your time and effort. Donate blood if you can. Call or visit a sick friend. Write thank-you notes.
- Involve your child in baking cookies for a new neighbor.
- Treat the environment and the creatures within it with kindness. Children who learn gentleness toward animals can often express the same caring attitude toward people.

Acts of Kindness

Make your child aware of acts of kindness around her. Always note when someone has paid you a kindness. For example, point out when someone holds a door open for you, or when a person makes room for you in traffic, or helps you pick up something you have dropped. Ask your child to tell you when someone has been kind to her. Remind your child that a caring person shows gratitude. Reinforce the message by sending thank-you notes to friends that have helped you out. Have your child make her own thank-you postcards by decorating or drawing a picture on one side of blank 3 x 5 index cards. Leave the other side blank for her message. The cards can be hand-delivered or stamped and mailed.

A Place to Care

Encourage caring by setting up a sick toy hospital in your home. Your child can fix toys, wash and clean dolls, or care for a sick teddy. When a teddy bear or stuffed animal, for example, is dropped, have your child bring him to the hospital for a check-up. Assign a drawer for supplies, or simply keep them in a small box. Include a mild soap for washing fabrics or washable toys, a soft-bristle brush, a small towel, a roll of plain gauze bandage, and perhaps a few adhesive bandages. Let your child know that you will provide sewing or "surgical services" when necessary. With your help, allow your child to make minor repairs based on her skill level.

Developing Caring

Caring for the needy

Explain to your child that not only are some adults homeless, but some children are homeless as well. Sometimes families with children have no place to live. One thing that such families often need is warm socks. If there is a homeless care center in your community, a donation of socks would most certainly be appreciated. You might wish to regularly pick up an extra package of socks when shopping at your discount store. Invite your child to choose the socks.

Let your child help you make sock puppets to donate as well. The puppets can be as simple or as elaborate as you like. Slip a sock over your child's hand and mark the place where eyes, nose and mouth would be. You can sew on buttons for the eyes and nose or simply use permanent marker to draw them on. Hair can be made from strands of yarn. Add a ribbon as a bow tie at the wrist or in the hair. Be sure to make an extra puppet for your child to keep.

Caring for Sick People

Invite your child to join you as you extend care to those who are sick. While it may not always be feasible or helpful for your child to visit a sick person, there are things he or she can do to say "I Care."

- Do you make chicken soup or some other special food when someone is ill? Let your child help out.
- Have your child make a Get Well card for a sick friend, grandparent, or teacher. Provide stickers, markers, and colored paper.

- Tape record your child singing a song and extending get-well wishes to a sick person.
- Let your child make a "care package" for a sick schoolmate. It could include an inexpensive storybook and a small stuffed animal.
- Invite your child to join you when you are helping someone who is ill by such actions as bringing in their garbage cans, raking their leaves, or shoveling their driveway.

Developing Character in Your Preschooler

Developing Caring

Caring in a Crisis

Explain to your child that sometimes people need extra help. Point out local news stories about victims of natural disasters. Let your child know that some people don't have a place to live or enough to eat. Explain that even by helping in small ways, he can make a difference. Set up a special savings jar or piggybank. Work out a system that involves your child in earning money to put in the jar. For example, if he cleans his room or eats all his vegetables, you will give him a dime to put in the jar. When the jar has enough money to make a purchase, take your child to the supermarket and help him purchase canned and dry goods for donation to a community food bank.

Big News

Create a family newsletter that highlights ways members of your family show that they care. This will help communicate to your youngster how much you value the character trait of caring. The complexity of the newsletter is up to you. It can be as simple as one sheet of paper—printed or handwritten. With your child, come up with a title for your newsletter. Your preschooler can help you keep track of story ideas and help to illustrate them. Reinforce the point of valuing kindness by looking in the local newspaper with your child and reading stories together about good deeds that people have done.

A Smile Shows You Care

Tell your youngster that you don't always have to do big things to show you care. Sometimes something as simple as a smile can make someone feel a little better. Encourage your child to smile and greet people with whom he or she comes into contact. This can be at home, at preschool, in the market, at the library, and so on. Explain to your child that taking time to smile and greet the people who are part of our lives lets them know that we value them and do not take them for granted. You can model this for your child by doing the same to the people with whom you come into contact. Not smiling or acknowledging someone can subtly communicate that we do not care enough to take the trouble to notice their presence.

Developing Character in Your Preschooler

Good citizens do their share to help their local communities, their states, their countries, and the world community. Good citizens cooperate with others, obey rules and laws, study and learn from past and present events, take care of the environment, respect authority, and are considerate neighbors.

A good citizen understands the importance of working to make life better for everyone in the community. Good citizens care about and pursue the common good. They participate in making things better by voicing their opinions, voting, serving on committees, reporting wrongdoing, and paying taxes. They understand and respect the principles of democracy. Good citizens also work to preserve and protect the environment.

Participation is the key to being a good citizen. Good citizens get involved in a variety of ways and stay involved.

> **Signs of Good Citizenship**
> Praise your child when he or she:
> - Is respectful to a teacher, coach, or other authority figure
> - Puts litter in a trash can in a public place
> - Wears a helmet when riding a bike or roller skating
> - Turns off the light when leaving a room
> - Recycles

Meet Kupa the Bear

Introduce your child to Kupa to help develop concepts about citizenship. Begin by showing Kupa's picture; then encourage conversation with these comments and questions:

- What kind of animal is Kupa? Did you know that bears live in different places all over the world?
- Kupa is a good citizen. A citizen is someone who lives in a certain place and is part of the community. Kupa thinks of herself as a citizen of the world.
- Where do you live? Did you know you are a citizen of the places where you live?
- Kupa is a good neighbor. She obeys the rules and laws. What are some rules you obey?
- Do you know what it means to cooperate? It means to work together to get things done or reach a goal. Kupa is always ready to do her share of the work.
- Kupa thinks that it is very important that everyone cooperate to take care of the environment. That means the Earth and everything in it. Can you think of some ways to take care of the Earth?

Developing Citizenship

Modeling Good Citizenship

You are a citizen of a family, a neighborhood, a community, a country, and the world. You can model citizenship at every level.

- Be a volunteer at your local school or community center. As little as one hour a week sets an example for your child and shows that you take your citizenship seriously.
- Protect the environment by conserving resources such as water and energy, and by recycling. When hiking or visiting a park, leave the area as clean (or cleaner) than when you arrived. If trash cans are not available, carry the trash out with you.
- Don't dispose of trash, oil, or paint in a storm drain.
- Be conscientious about playing by the rules. Respect teachers, coaches, police officers, and others who have been given authority.
- Exercise your right to vote. Make sure your child knows that you voted on Voting Day.
- Take an interest in other cultures. Read and share stories about other cultures with your child.

The Strength of a Community

Ask your child if he or she knows what a community is. Help your child understand that a community is a group of people living in the same place under the same laws. Talk together about some of the different members of your local community—home owners, shop keepers, law enforcement and safety officials, teachers, the mayor, council members, and so on. Give your child one toothpick and ask him to break it. He should be able to do so. Then give your child a dozen toothpicks in a bunch and ask him to break them all together. He won't accomplish this. Tell your youngster that by working together, people within a community are stronger and can accomplish more than they could by themselves. For example, explain that by pooling financial resources through taxes, people are able to have police protection, community centers, and so on. However, one family would not be able to pay for the police or the community center alone.

Developing Citizenship

Recycling Helps Earth

Good citizens care for and protect the environment. Recycling is a good, earth-friendly habit to encourage in your child. On trash day have your child help you gather up and dispose of the family trash. Explain what happens to it once it is picked up and where it goes. Point out that some things are used only once, but many items made of glass, paper and plastic can be recycled and used again. Talk together about how this helps the environment. Work with your child to find earth-friendly ways to dispose of discarded toys. Many are made of recyclable materials. If the toy is unbroken, help your child clean it up and donate it to a facility that can put it to good use.

Community History

Does your community have a heritage center? If not you can probably find out about your town's history at the library. Make it a fun project with your youngster as the two of you learn more about your hometown. How was it founded? When was the first school built? Are there any historic sites that you can visit together? Tell your youngster that a good citizen is interested in knowing about past events that helped mold and establish the community, country, and world in which we live.

People in Charge

Explain to your child that people in authority have important jobs to do. They cannot do their jobs unless everyone else cooperates with them. Explain that a good citizen respects authority. Here's a fun way to talk more about what it means to be in authority. Ask your child to draw pictures of these people who protect or serve the community—police officers, fire fighters, sheriffs, teachers, and coaches. Help your child cut out the pictures and use them to make puppets by gluing them to craft sticks, strips of stiff cardboard, or cardboard tubes (such as paper towel rolls). Use the figures as you explain that during a day at school, teachers have authority in the classroom. They make decisions based on their experience and knowledge of what is best for all of the students. For everyone to get the best out of a school day, they must listen to and respect the teacher's decisions. Coaches represent authority during a game or practice. Continue in this manner, explaining the importance of the authority of law enforcement officers and fire fighters.

Developing Citizenship

Problem-Solving Tools

Remind your child that a good citizen is always ready to do his or her share. Let your child know that even youngsters can work at solving problems and helping others. Explain that the Six Pillars of Character—trustworthiness, respect, responsibility, fairness, caring, and citizenship—are tools your child can use. You can help your child visualize this by making a "tool box" together. A plastic tool kit from a store, or hand-drawn cardboard tools in a shoebox work equally well. Just be sure that there are six tools. Use a marker to label each with one of the Six Pillars of Character. If desired, your child can draw the matching animal's face on the opposite side of each tool. When a problem arises, have your child get the tool box and look through it. Ask "What do we need to solve this problem? Can we use fairness, caring, or respect?" Let your child decide what will work and then talk about how to apply the "tool."

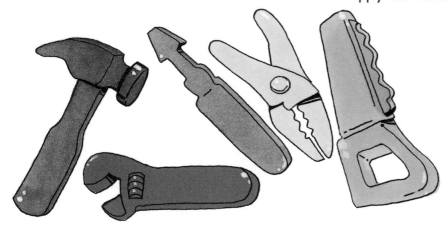

Enjoying Our Home

To encourage a concern for the environment, take your child for a walk. Bring along gloves and a trash bag if you would like to be prepared to clean up any litter you might find. To make your walk even more exciting, search for evidence of animal life such as chewed leaves, webs, nests, or tracks. Gather soil samples in cups. Bring them home and water them to see if hidden seeds might sprout. If your walk takes you through a grassy field, check your socks when you return home. They are a perfect collection device for a wide variety of sticky seeds. Ask your child what the world would be like if there were no natural places left to enjoy.

Be Sure to Vote

The next time you have the opportunity to vote, explain the process to your child. Let her see the ways that you gather information about the candidates and proposals. Do you decide based on reading the newspaper, listening to commercials, watching debates, reading voting guides, or all of the above? Take your child to the polls when they are not crowded, and ask if she might be allowed to see the inside of a booth. You may also wish to create a voting situation at home that involves the entire family. You might have the family vote about what you should have for Saturday dinner. Explain the elements needed to make a well-balanced meal, then have each family member make suggestions. Conduct a vote by a show of hands or by ballot. You can also involve your child and her friends in voting for kid's choice awards. Let them vote for their favorite animal, food, cartoon character, and so on.

Developing Character in Your Preschooler

My CHARACTER COUNTS! Chart

Look for times when your child demonstrates each of the "Six Pillars of Character." Let your child color a corresponding medal each time you "catch" him or her behaving properly.

Developing Character in Your Preschooler